W9-CNA-353

The Skateboarder's Guide to
Skate Parks, Half-Pipes, Bowls, and Obstacles™

RIPPIN' RAMPS

A Skateboarder's Guide to Riding Half-Pipes

Justin Hocking

The Rosen Publishing Group, Inc., New York

For Matt and Sean

Published in 2005 by The Rosen Publishing Group, Inc.
29 East 21st Street, New York, NY 10010

Library of Congress Cataloging-in-Publication Data

Hocking, Justin.
Rippin' ramps: a skateboarder's guide to riding half-pipes/by Justin Hocking.
   p. cm.—(The skateboarder's guide to skate parks, half-pipes, bowls,
   and obstacles)
Includes bibliographical references and index.
ISBN 1-4042-0340-0 (library binding)
1. Skateboarding–Juvenile literature.
I. Title.
GV859.8.H62 2004
796.22—dc22

               2004004391

Manufactured in the United States of America

On the cover: A skateboarder doing a frontside 5-0 grind on a quarter-pipe.

CONTENTS

INTRODUCTION

The chances are pretty good that you've seen one at your local skate park or in your favorite video games. Maybe you've noticed one on TV, too, and you watched in amazement as professional skateboarders used it to launch 15 feet (4.6 meters) in the air. Or maybe someone in your neighborhood has one tucked away in his or her own backyard. Maybe your town even has a local skate park where some of the best skaters around come and perform their best tricks.

At the X Games, shown here, skaters compete on some of the most innovative half-pipes in the world. These half-pipes allow professional skateboarders to perform some of their most daring tricks.

Half-pipes are everywhere. They're at public skate parks, in professional contests like *Thrasher* magazine's Boost Mobile Invitational or the X Games, and in the backyards of skateboarders all over the world.

But if you're like a lot of younger skaters, you're not totally sure how to ride them. Or maybe you already know the basics, but you want to learn some harder tricks. Half-pipes are great for jumping to the next level of skateboarding. You can do tricks on half-pipes that you can't do on the street. These tricks include airs and rock-and-rolls, which we'll discuss later.

No matter what level you're at, this book has something for you, from step-by-step instructions on the basics of riding half-pipes, to some more advanced tricks. We'll also give you some helpful tips for doing what skateboarding is really all about—having fun with your friends. So grab your board and get ready to rip the half-pipe!

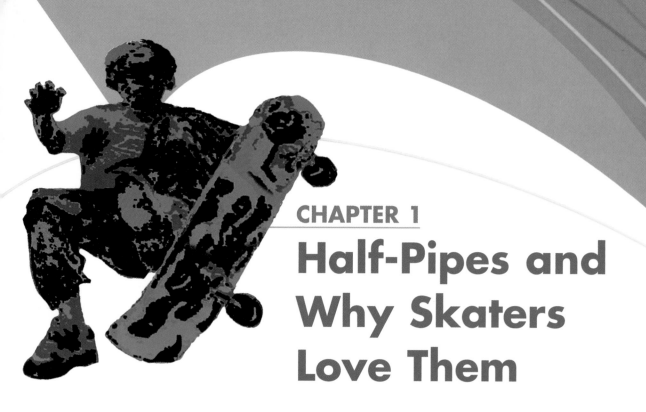

CHAPTER 1
Half-Pipes and Why Skaters Love Them

If you're familiar with the world of professional skateboarding, you know that street skating is popular with professional skateboarders these days. Almost all skateboarders, both amateurs and pros (or professionals, who are skateboarders who get paid to skateboard), love the freedom and thrill of rolling through streets, parking lots, and plazas and doing tricks on "natural" obstacles such as benches and stairs.

But a lot of pro skaters will tell you that some of their most memorable skate sessions took place on half-pipes. Why is this? Because there's an incredible sense of exhilaration you get from rolling on a half-pipe's smoothly curving surface, similar to the feeling a surfer gets from riding a perfect wave. And unlike a lot of street spots where you're more likely to get kicked out if you skate in a large group, half-pipes

Before skating on half-pipes, it is important to know the different parts of these ramps. The curved sections, shown here facing each other, are called the transitions. At the top, or the lip, of the ramp is metal piping called coping. Coping allows skaters to slide and grind their boards across the lip. Ramps are often surfaced with plywood. The plywood is then covered with a smooth wood called Masonite or other smooth materials such as Skatelite.

are a great place for a bigger crew of skaters to get together and have a skate session.

The Parts of a Half-Pipe

Before you hop on a half-pipe, it's important to know the names of all the different half-pipe elements. Most half-pipes are made of plywood and then surfaced with a smooth material called Masonite. Masonite wears out pretty quickly though, so newer, more weather-resistant surfaces such as Skatelite, a plastic-based surface, are becoming popular.

The curved sections of the half-pipe are called transitions, trannys, or walls. Most half-pipes have two transitions facing one another, which can vary in size and steepness. The horizontal part of the half-pipe that sits just above the ground separating the two transitions is called the flat-bottom. Most half-pipes have at least 12 feet (3.7 m) of flatbottom, which gives you plenty of time to set up for tricks between walls.

At the top of each transition is a round metal pipe called the coping, which sits on the top, or the lip, of the ramp. The coping is a surface for doing grinds and stalls, and it helps you pop out (bounce your wheels off the coping for extra height) on aerial tricks.

Finally, sitting on top of each transition you'll find the decks. This is where skaters chill out between runs.

Half-Pipe Extras

Some half-pipes have added features that make them more fun and challenging to skate. Sometimes skaters want an extra few feet of height on the top of a small section of their half-pipe, so they'll add what's called an extension or a tombstone.

If the lip of an extension angles down until it reaches the normal height of the half-pipe, this is called an escalator. Just like the escalator in the mall can take you from the second floor to the first floor, a half-pipe escalator allows you to grind smoothly from an extension down to the lower part of the half-pipe's lip.

A sloping passage that connects the deck to the transition, cutting away the lip, is called a roll in or a channel.

A spine is where two complete half-pipes are set back-to-back, so that their copings are welded together at the top. This allows skaters to grind or air from one half-pipe to the other.

GIRL POWER

There aren't as many girl skaters as boy skaters. But girls often find that half-pipes are a good place to start developing basic balance and coordination on a skateboard. Some female professionals, including Cara-Beth Burnside and Jen O'Brien, have even made a career out of skating half-pipes.

Every day more and more girls are beginning to skate. So don't be shy. You can pick up some half-pipe basics in just a day or two, even if you're just starting out.

A hip is created when two half-pipes are placed next to one another and at a slight angle. A hip also allows skaters to transfer from one half-pipe to the other.

Types of Half-Pipes

Most half-pipes are unique in some way, but there are two main varieties: the mini (miniature) half-pipe and the vert (vertical) half-pipe. Mini half-pipes are a good place to learn basic tricks. They're usually somewhere between 2 feet (0.6 m) and 8 feet (2.4 m) tall, with transitions that are fairly easy to maneuver.

Vert half-pipes are much taller. They're usually between 9 and 13 feet (2.7 and 4 m) high. Vert half-pipes typically have about 9 feet (2.7 m) of transition, and at least 1 foot (0.3 m) of vertical, or vert, at the top, just below the coping. This is why they're called "vert" half-pipes.

Mind Your Manners

Your parents taught you your manners, right? Skateboarders have manners, too, and there are some important ones you need to know about at half-pipes and public skate parks. Manners are especially important on a half-pipe because they help keep you and others safe. Here's a list of the three most important manners you need to know about:

1. **Watch and Learn:** When you show up to a new half-pipe or skate park, spend some time watching people skate before you even step on your own board. Pay attention to the way experienced skateboarders use the half-pipe, and watch to see what lines they take. Watching the masters will help you learn, and also help you avoid accidents and collisions.
2. **Wait Your Turn:** When skating a half-pipe, wait your turn, or else you might get called a snake. (A snake is someone who doesn't wait his or her turn and cuts other skaters off. It's definitely not cool to be a snake.) Never drop in on a half-pipe in the middle of someone else's run. And keep your board out of the drop-in position (the position where you place your trucks and wheels out on the coping) whenever someone else is skating.
3. **Don't Hog the Half-Pipe:** If the half-pipe is crowded, don't spend too much time on one run. Make a few turns and then let someone else go. Don't worry, you'll get plenty of time to skate.

Keeping It Safe

So you're ready for a half-pipe session, right? Well, almost. You need to know just a couple more things about safety, and then you'll be good to go.

When skating a half-pipe, you must wear top-of-the-line knee and elbow pads (we'll talk more about how to use your pads and helmet in the next chapter).

The most important thing to do before stepping onto any ramp is to gear up in the proper padding. The various types of protective gear include elbow pads *(top left)* and knee pads *(bottom left)*. Since falling on a half-pipe involves sliding down the transition on your knees, and sometimes on your elbows, you'll be glad that you have these pads. The most important protective gear you can wear is your helmet *(right)*.

Probably the best way of staying safe, though, is to skate at your own pace. It can be intimidating when there are lots of experienced skaters around. You might feel pressured to try tricks that are beyond your abilities. Skateboarding involves taking risks and pushing yourself. But remember that it's not about competition or showing up other skaters. It's about moving at your own learning pace. It's an incredible feeling when you learn something new, even if it's very basic. Don't worry about what other people think. And don't try to show off too much at first (you can save that for later, once you start really ripping). Take it slow and progress at your own level, and you'll be sure to have many fun years of skateboarding ahead of you.

CHAPTER 2
Getting Started

As we mentioned in the previous chapter, it's essential that you wear a pair of good skateboard-specific knee pads, elbow pads, and a helmet when skating, especially on a half-pipe. Companies like Rector, Protec, and Boneless all make top-of-the-line pads, the kind with a thick plastic cap over the kneecap.

If you've seen lots of people skate a half-pipe, then you know exactly what this cap is for: when experienced skaters fall, instead of flopping like a dead fish to the bottom of the half-pipe, they drop to their knees and slide gracefully down the transition on their knee pads. Before you start actually skating a half-pipe, it's a good idea to practice some knee slides.

Knee Slide

No matter how good a skater you are, you're going to occasionally fall. And the safest way to fall on a ramp is to slide down on your knees. Once you've

1 Run a few feet up the transition of the half-pipe.

2 As you near the top of the half-pipe, turn around and fall to your knees.

3 Slide down the transition on your knee pads with your feet dragging beneath you. Place some weight on your feet beneath you, but avoid sitting down too hard on your heels, which could lead to an ankle or foot injury.

4 As you slide, lean back a little. If you start to fall forward, instead of putting your hands out in front of you and risking an arm or wrist injury, fall onto your elbow pads and use them to slide, the same way you slide on your knee pads. It's sort of an awkward position, but you'll get used to it.

(continued on page 14)

Knee Slide (continued)

Wait until you stop sliding, get back up, and start skating again.

5

gotten the hang of this, try working your way higher up the half-pipe and doing longer slides.

Pumping

Now that you know how to fall, it's time to learn the most basic element of skating a half-pipe: pumping. Pumping is the action that keeps you moving on a half-pipe instead of slowly coming to a stop. It's what gives advanced skaters the momentum to take those long runs, linking trick after trick after trick. Just as you had to slowly learn how to walk long before you ever set foot on a skateboard, it's essential that you learn to pump before you learn how to drop in. Pumping feels a little weird at first. It's a completely new kind of movement, and it takes some getting used to. But stick with it, and you'll be doing it in no time. Another important thing to know is that it's easier to pump on a slightly bigger half-pipe. The transitions on a bigger half-pipe are usually a little less steep, and you don't have to worry about hitting the coping once you start getting higher.

The secret to pumping is pressing down on your board as you skate up and down the transitions of the half-pipe. Pressing down on your board as you go up and as you come down each transition is sort of like pressing down on a gas pedal in a car. When you apply downward force with your legs and feet, you pick up speed (major speed if you push hard enough).

Keep in mind that all the pumping motion comes from your legs. So make sure to bend with your knees. And instead of hunching over too much, keep your upper-body pretty much vertical. You can think of pumping as a sort of one-two rhythmic motion. You pump once as you go up each transition, and then you pump again as you come down, one-two, one-two. Here's a step-by-step instruction:

 Start off by standing on your board on the flat bottom. Start pushing toward the opposite wall. As you put your back foot back on the board, make sure your feet are aligned and that your weight is evenly spread between both feet.

 Approach the transition with your knees slightly bent.

 Once you reach the transition, use the energy in your bent knees to stand up a little bit while you press down on the skateboard as you move up the transition. Make sure to press down evenly with both feet.

PUMPING

(continued on page 16)

15

4 Avoid leaning toward the wall as you travel up the transition. If anything, lean back a bit toward the flat bottom so that your body remains perpendicular to the skateboard. As you travel up the wall, bend your knees again slightly.

5 As you begin to roll back down the transition, don't turn the skateboard. Simply turn your head in the direction you're moving and look where you're going. Press down on the board again as you roll back through the transition.

Keep working on pumping until you can get higher and higher and hold your speed in the half-pipe. It takes a while, but eventually you'll get it. Set small goals for yourself. For instance, you might pick out a sticker or a row of screw-heads toward the top of the half-pipe and try to touch it with your front wheels. Once you start getting close to the lip of the half-pipe, you're probably ready for the next step: dropping in.

Dropping In

Your first time dropping in can be a little scary, but it's also one of the more thrilling things you'll do on a skateboard. Now that you know how to pump, dropping in is really pretty simple. But before you learn any other tricks on a half-pipe, you have to drop in first. Starting from the top of the half-pipe is the only way to get enough speed to set up for other tricks. The sequence on the next page shows you how to do it.

1 Set your tail down on the coping of the half-pipe with the trucks and wheels hanging over the edge. Place your back foot on the tail to keep the board in place. Keep your knees slightly bent.

2 Slowly move your front foot forward, keeping most of your weight on your back foot. Rest your front foot at a slight forward angle over your front bolts, and keep your knees bent.

3 Now begin to lean forward, shifting much of your weight forward. Avoid the urge to lean backward. As your hips begin to move forward, straighten your front leg out a little. Push the nose of your board down into the half-pipe so that your front wheels touch the transition.

4 Keep your knees bent slightly and ride down to the flat bottom. Congratulations on performing your first drop in!

DROPPING IN

VISUALIZATION

Ask any pro skater and they'll tell you that skateboarding takes just as much mental effort and imagination as it does physical skill. Before you try any new trick, picture yourself doing it in your head. Go through each motion as if you were watching yourself in a movie. See yourself landing the trick perfectly.

Imagine your foot position, how it will feel when you land, etc. Really see yourself riding away clean. If it helps, imagine very specific details such as the color of your shirt and the sound of your friends cheering after you land.

Once you actually go for the trick, say to yourself "I can do this." Eventually you will. For a slight variation, imagine your favorite pro skater landing the trick, and then try to imitate his or her style.

Though the knee slide, pumping, and dropping in seem like very basic techniques on the half-pipe, they are probably the most important things to learn when first getting started. Without these techniques, you won't be able to move on to the more advanced tricks like grinds, slides, and airs, which we'll soon cover.

CHAPTER 3
Basic Half-Pipe Tricks

N ow that you can pump and drop in on a half-pipe, it's time to start learning some basic tricks. At this point, you probably only know how to go forward and backward on the half-pipe. Now you need to figure out how to move around and use the whole ramp.

Kick Turn

The best way to move around on a half-pipe is by learning how to turn the board with a trick called a kick turn. Most people start out learning backside kick turns. Once you get the hang of going backside, try some frontside turns, or turns that are in the direction of your heels. It's the same motion, only you have to look over your lead shoulder as you turn. The sequence on the next page shows you how to do them.

KICK TURN

 Ride up the transition with your knees slightly bent.

 As you approach the lip, lift up your back heel just slightly and press down on your tail with your toe. This helps you lift up your front trucks and wheels just slightly off the half-pipe surface.

With your lead shoulder slightly tucked, turn your lead hip and shoulder 180 degrees, until they're pointing in the direction of the opposite wall of the half-pipe. (For a backside kick turn, turn in the direction of your toes. For a frontside turn, turn in the direction of your heels.)

 Pump the transition as you come back down and prepare for the next wall.

Kick turns are a great foundation trick, because once you get them, you'll have no problem doing some other simple tricks, like grinds.

Grind

A simple grind is really nothing more than a kick turn, except your back truck makes contact with the coping. Here's how to do it:

Approach the wall at a slight angle, either backside or frontside, with enough speed to reach the lip of the half-pipe.

As you start to make your kick turn, raise your back heel and use the toes on your back foot to put a little extra pressure on the edge of your tail. This makes it easier for your back wheel to lap, or ride over, the coping so your truck will grind the lip.

As your back truck hits the coping, shift some of your weight to your back foot. Make sure you lean forward as you grind and keep your body leaning into the half-pipe.

(continued on page 22)

4 As you complete your grind, again put some pressure on the edge of your tail. This will help to get your back truck and wheel smoothly off the coping.

5 Keep your knees bent and ride down the wall.

Axle Stall

Once you get the hang of simple grinds (some people call them scratcher grinds, because you're basically just scratching the coping), you can start thinking about axle stalls. "Axle" is another name for your trucks, so when you do an axle stall, you rest both trucks (along with your whole body) on the top of the coping, rather than grinding.

Axle stalls are another important foundation trick, and they lead to some of the intermediate tricks (like the 50-50) that we'll talk about in the next chapter.

The axle stall is a basic trick in which both axles rest on top of the coping. The axle stall is good because it allows you to pause for a moment to help you set up for your next trick or to simply rest. The sequence on the next pages shows you how to do them. The axle stall

For an axle stall, unlike a grind, you want to make a straight-line approach to the lip. You don't need to go at an angle because you won't be moving across the coping. You also need some extra speed to get all the way on top of the deck.

As you reach the top of the half-pipe, press down on your tail and lift up your front truck so that it doesn't hit the coping.

Set your back truck on the coping first, putting some extra weight on your back heel so you can get your board and body all the way up on the deck.

Once your back truck is resting on the coping, use it to pivot your shoulders and hips around so they're in line with the coping below you.

(continued on page 24)

5 Set your front trucks down, keeping the weight on your heels and your body leaning in toward the half-pipe.

6 After you stall for a second, press down on your tail with the toes of your back foot, lean forward, turn off the coping, and ride back into the half-pipe.

allows you to move on to more advanced tricks, like the 50-50 grind discussed later.

Tail Stall

Another simple stall you can try is the tail stall, also called the tail tap. If you can drop in and pump, then tail stalls will come pretty naturally because they involve the exact same motions as dropping in.

Like axle stalls, tail stalls are a good set up trick. It gives you a chance to get set for more difficult tricks. While the goal with a tail stall is to ride up backward, set your tail down on the coping, and then rest for a second on the lip, you can work your way up by tapping your tail below the coping (on the half-pipe surface) a few times, just for practice. The sequence on the next page shows you how to do the tail stall.

1 Approach the wall going backward (riding backward is also called going fakie) with enough speed to reach the lip.

2 As you approach the coping, bend your knees and press down on your tail with the ball of your foot.

3 Straighten out your back leg, jamming your tail up on to the coping and the deck. As your back leg straightens out, your front knee should bend up toward your torso.

4 Stall on your tail for just a second, getting your body all the way up on the deck. You can grab the nose of the board if you want.

(continued on page 26)

Tail Stall
(continued)

 5

Now straighten out your front leg and press down on your front foot, just like dropping in!

Rock-and-Roll to Fakie

A good trick to do after you drop in from your tail stall, and another important basic trick, is the rock-and-roll to fakie. When you do a regular rock-and-roll, you jam your front trucks and wheels up over the coping and then turn backside into the half-pipe. But with a rock-and-roll to fakie, you come backward down the wall.

One good way to warm up for a rock-and-roll to fakie is to ride up the wall below the lip and lifting your front trucks and wheels slightly off the half-pipe, like you're doing a little manual, or a wheelie, just below the coping. Here's how to do the rock-and-roll to fakie:

ROCK-AND-ROLL
TO FAKIE

1

Ride straight up the transition, leaning back just slightly.

As you approach the lip, press down on the tail with your back foot, lifting your front trucks and wheels over the coping.

3

Set the center of your board down on the coping by straightening out your front leg and using your foot to press your front truck and wheels down on the deck. At the same time, bend your back knee.

4

As you stall, shift your weight to the outside edge of your back foot, so that the inside edge of your foot lifts up slightly. Use the outside edge to press down on the tail and lift your truck and wheels back over the coping.

5

Set your front trucks back down on the half-pipe, and shift some of your weight to your front foot. As you roll backward down the half-pipe, turn your head and look directly toward the opposite wall.

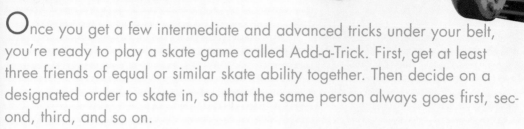

HOW TO PLAY "ADD-A-TRICK"

Once you get a few intermediate and advanced tricks under your belt, you're ready to play a skate game called Add-a-Trick. First, get at least three friends of equal or similar skate ability together. Then decide on a designated order to skate in, so that the same person always goes first, second, third, and so on.

To begin the game, the first skater drops in and does a trick. The next skater has to do that trick, and also add another trick. The skater after that has to do the first two tricks, and add a trick of his or her own, and so on. As soon as anyone misses one trick in the sequence, they're out. Things get pretty fun (and pretty hectic) after a few rounds, once you have to do five or more tricks in a row. The last person to complete the run and add a new trick, wins.

The basic half-pipe tricks like the kick turn, grind, axle stall, tail stall, and rock-and-roll to fakie are all designed to help you move on to more advanced tricks. By learning them, you've partially learned how to do the more advanced tricks already.

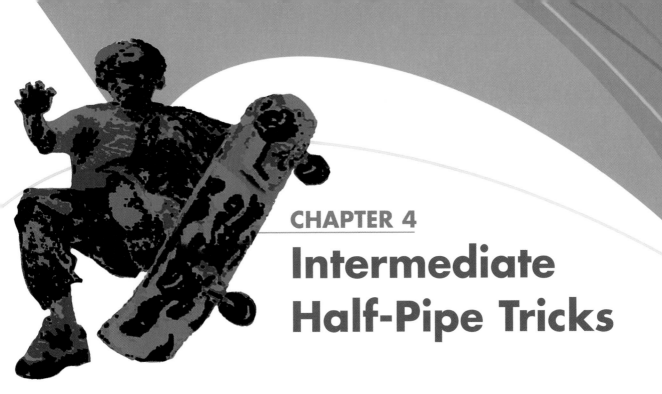

CHAPTER 4
Intermediate Half-Pipe Tricks

S o now that you can do some basic tricks like axle stalls and rock-and-rolls to fakies, you're getting hungry to try some harder moves. By this point, you're probably starting to go a little faster on the half-pipe. That's good. You'll need the extra speed for this next round of high-powered tricks.

50-50 Grind

One trick that definitely takes a little more speed is the 50-50 grind. The 50-50 grind is an essential trick. It helps you get speed for highly advanced tricks like airs and inverts. A 50-50 grind involves almost the same motions as an axle stall, except you actually grind across the coping instead of just stalling. The sequence on the next page shows you how to do them.

1 Approach the coping as you would for an axle stall, except with more speed and at more of an angle.

2 Similar to when you're doing an axle stall, lift your front truck and begin grinding on your back truck. Once your back truck is firmly on the coping, set down your front truck.

3 As you grind on both trucks, put pressure on both your heels, so that you stay up on the deck. But, at the same time, keep your body weight and waist in toward the half-pipe so you don't roll out, and so you're ready to drop back in.

4 As you complete your grind, press down on your tail with the ball of your back foot, while turning your hips and shoulders back into the half-pipe.

5 Keep your knees bent slightly as you drop back in and head toward the opposite wall.

Boardslide

Just like 50-50s are an easy step up from the axle stall, the boardslide is just an advanced form of the rock-and-roll to fakie. Instead of just stalling, though, you actually slide across the coping on the bottom of your board. Here's how to do the boardslide:

1 Approach the wall as if you were going to do a rock-and-roll to fakie, except with much more speed and at more of an angle to the coping. The angle will give you the momentum to slide, rather than just stall.

2 As you set the center of your board on the coping, put enough weight on your front foot so that your back wheels lift off the surface of the half-pipe, making it possible for you to slide.

(continued on page 32)

31

3 Press down on the balls of your feet, making the center of your board slide across the coping.

4 As you near the end of the slide, lift up the inside edge of your back foot. Press down on the tail with the outside edge of your back foot, and lift your truck and wheels back over the coping.

5 When you set your front trucks and wheels back down on the half-pipe, put some extra weight on your front foot. Turn your head and look over your lead shoulder as you roll backward toward the flat bottom. Keep your knees bent to absorb your weight as you hit the transition.

Now that you've got some basic grinds and slides, you're probably getting the natural urge to go above and beyond the coping. As you know, half-pipes are the best place for doing airs. In fact the world records for the highest airs were set on a half-pipe. But before you start going head-high, you have to learn the basis for all airs: the ollie.

Ollie

Before you try ollies on a half-pipe, make sure you're first able to do them on the street. Also, unlike most grinds and slides, most people find that frontside ollies are easier to learn first. Here's how to do them:

1 Approach the lip at a slight angle, with your knees bent and your weight on the balls of your feet.

2 Just like you would for a street ollie, snap your tail with the ball of your back foot so that it hits the surface of the half-pipe.

3 As the board begins to rise, push the outside edge of your front foot forward to lift your nose and guide the board up into the air.

OLLIE

(continued on page 34)

Ollie (continued)

4 As your board rises into the air, lift your knees up toward your chest.

5 As you start coming back into the half-pipe, focus on your landing spot.

6 Straighten your legs out a bit, landing toward the top of the transition with your knees slightly bent and both of your feet flat on the board.

Tail Slide

Once you get the ollie down, you're ready for the most difficult of the intermediate tricks: the tail slide. Again, like the ollie, most people start out doing tail slides in the frontside direction. Before you try this trick, you should be able to do frontside 180 ollies on flat ground. The sequence on the next page shows you how to do the tail slide.

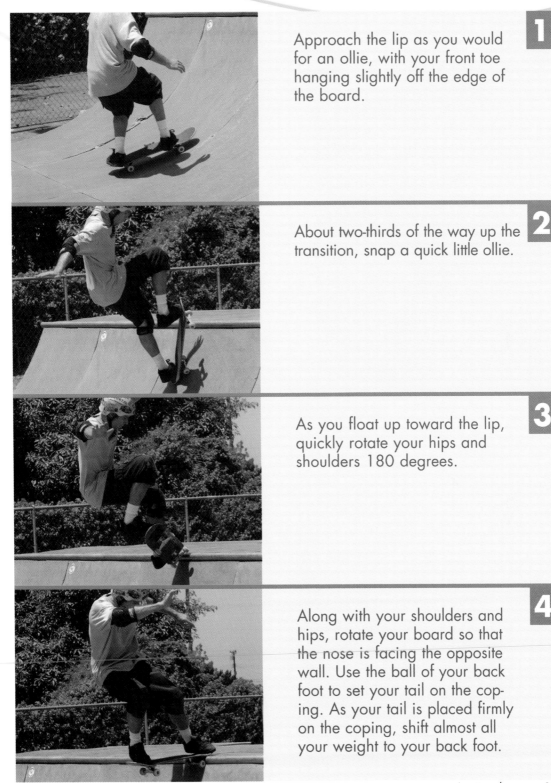

1 Approach the lip as you would for an ollie, with your front toe hanging slightly off the edge of the board.

2 About two-thirds of the way up the transition, snap a quick little ollie.

3 As you float up toward the lip, quickly rotate your hips and shoulders 180 degrees.

4 Along with your shoulders and hips, rotate your board so that the nose is facing the opposite wall. Use the ball of your back foot to set your tail on the coping. As your tail is placed firmly on the coping, shift almost all your weight to your back foot.

(continued on page 36)

Tail Slide
(continued)

5 Keeping your knees bent, press down firmly on your tail with your back foot, making it slide smoothly across the lip. Keep your knees bent and stay right on top of your board as you slide.

6 Just before your slide starts to end, drop back into the half-pipe.

Now that you've learned the intermediate half-pipe tricks, you've built a solid foundation for the hardest tricks in this book. These include airs, rock-and-rolls, blunts, and kick flips. You're on your way to becoming a seasoned professional.

CHAPTER 5

Advanced Half-Pipe Tricks

Now that you have some intermediate tricks under your belt, you're ready to step it up a few notches. The following four tricks can be pretty tough, but they're all really just variations on the basic and intermediate tricks you've learned. Keep in mind that it takes most skaters a long time to learn these advanced tricks. If you start to get frustrated, remember the three Ps: persistence, patience, and practice.

Frontside Air

If you're comfortable with the ollie, frontside airs, or aerials, will come pretty naturally. An air is basically just a big ollie in which you grab the board with your hand.

FRONTSIDE AIR

 1

Ride up the transition the same way you would for a frontside ollie, with your weight on the balls of your feet and your knees bent.

2

Press down on your tail with your back foot and snap an ollie (if you're on a vert half-pipe, you really don't need to snap your tail because you'll go straight into the air anyway).

3

As your board pops up, lift your knees up toward your body. Reach down to the board with your back hand and grab a comfortable spot on the deck.

4

As you start to come down, spot your landing, just like you would for a frontside ollie.

Avoid the urge to hang on to your board too long. Let go before you set the board down, and bend your knees a bit for the landing.

Frontside Rock-and-Roll

The frontside rock-and-roll is a classic trick. A frontside rock-and-roll is just like a rock-and-roll to fakie, but instead of coming in backward you come back in frontside.

When done properly, it is one of the more stylish moves you can do on a skateboard. Here's how to do it:

1 Roll up the wall at a slight frontside angle, leaning back slightly.

2 Press down on your tail and rest the center of your board on the coping. Remember to straighten your front leg and press your front wheels down on the deck with your front foot, which will make your back wheels rock up, or lift up off the surface of the half-pipe.

(continued on page 40)

3 As you press your front wheels down on the deck, look directly over your front shoulder at the transition. Also, the secret to frontside rock-and-rolls is arching your back as you look over your shoulder, which will make it easier to come back down the transition.

4 Press down on the tail with the outside edge of your back foot, and lift your front trucks and wheels over the coping. As you do this, keep your back knee bent and try bowing your legs out a bit, looking over your shoulder the whole time.

5 Set your front trucks and wheels back on the half-pipe and ride back down the transition.

Ollie Blunt

Also known as just the blunt, this is one of the more technically advanced tricks done on the lip of the half-pipe. A blunt is a trick in which you stall with your back truck and tail on the lip, and then ollie back into the half-pipe. Warm up with a few simple ollie to fakies and then move on to ollie blunts. The sequence on the next pages shows you how to do an ollie blunt.

 1 Ride straight up the transition toward the lip, like you would for a rock-and-roll to fakie. You don't need a lot of speed for this trick. Make sure you have all your weight on the balls of your feet and toes.

2 Just before your front wheels have the chance to hit the coping, press down on your tail with the ball of your back foot.

 3 Guide your back wheels up over the coping and onto the deck. Press firmly down on your tail, making your board stall on the coping.

  4 Now here's the most difficult part: to get out of the blunt stall position, you have to pop an ollie off the coping. Pop your tail with your back foot, and use the outside edge of your front foot to guide the board up and then back into the half-pipe.

OLLIE BLUNT

(continued on page 42)

Ollie Blunt
(continued)

Straighten your legs and ride back down the transition.

5

Frontside Kick Flip

Also known simply as a frontside flip, this is one of the most technically difficult tricks you can do on a half-pipe. In order to do this half-pipe trick, you should be really comfortable with ollies on a half-pipe, and you need to have kick flips wired on flat ground. Here's how to do a frontside kick flip:

FRONTSIDE KICK FLIP

Approach the lip at a slight frontside angle, like you would for a frontside ollie.

1

At the top of the half-pipe, pop a good-sized ollie.

2

3 As you ollie, drag the outside edge of you front foot up toward the upper edge of your nose. Use the side of your foot and toe to flick the board one full rotation.

4 After the flick, circle your front foot around the nose of your board, so that the board flips between your legs.

5 Catch the board on your feet and spot your landing over your front shoulder.

6 Bend your knees as you set the board down and ride it out.

GLOSSARY

backside Any trick in which you turn in the direction of your toes.

bail Falling off your skateboard.

fakie The position when you're riding backward on the board with your feet in your normal stance.

frontside Any trick in which you turn in the direction of your heels.

manual A trick in which you lift up your front trucks and you balance on your back wheels while riding. If you balance instead on your front wheels, it's called a nose manual. The manual is also sometimes called a wheelie.

session The gathering of a group of skaters.

snake Someone who doesn't wait his or her turn during a session and who takes way too many runs.

switchstance Usually just called a switch. This is when you do a trick with your feet in the opposite stance that you usually ride.

trucks Also called axles, they are the metal devices that hold your wheels to the board and make it possible to turn.

Skatelab Skateboarding Camp
4226 Valley Fair Street
Simi Valley, CA 93063
(805) 578-0040
Web site: http://www.skatelab.com

Vans Skateboard Camp
P.O. Box 368
Government Camp, OR 97028
(800) 334-4272
Web site: http://www.vansskatecamp.com

Woodward Camp
P.O. Box 93
134 Sports Camp Drive
Route 45
Woodward, PA 16882
(814) 349-5633
Web site: http://www.woodwardcamp.com

Web Sites

Due to the changing nature of Internet links, the Rosen Publishing Group, Inc., has developed an online list of Web sites related to the subject of this book. This site is updated regularly. Please use this link to access the list:

http://www.rosenlinks.com/skgu/rira

FOR FURTHER READING

Brooke, Michael. *The Concrete Wave: The History of Skateboarding.* Toronto, ON: Warwick Publishing, 1999.

Davis, Gary, and Craig Steycyk. *Dysfunctional.* Corte Madera, CA: Gingko Press, 1999.

Hawk, Tony. *Hawk: Occupation: Skateboarder.* New York: Reagan Books, 2000.

Thatcher, Kevin. *Thrasher Presents How to Build Skateboard Ramps: Halfpipes, Boxes, Bowls and More.* San Francisco: High Speed Productions, 2001.

Thrasher magazine. *Thrasher: Insane Terrain.* New York: Universe Publishing, 2001.

Weyland, Jocko. *The Answer Is Never.* New York: Grove Press, 2002.

BIBLIOGRAPHY

Pointx.com. "Contact Us." Retrieved January 24, 2004 (http://www.pointx.com/contact_us.asp).

Skateboard.com. "Camps." Retrieved January 24, 2004 (http://www.skateboard.com/frontside/GetLocal/camps/default.asp).

Skateboarding.com. "This Is the News 5.28.02." Retrieved January 23, 2004 (http://www.skateboarding.com/skate/news/article/0,12364,250225,00.html).

Vansskatecamp.com. "Skate—Summer 2004." Retrieved January 24, 2004 (http://www.vansskatecamp.com/index.htm).

INDEX

A
airs, 4, 8, 18, 29, 32, 36
axle stalls, 22–24, 28, 29, 31

B
boardslide, 31–32
Boneless company, 12

C
coping, 8, 9, 14, 16, 22, 24, 26, 29, 31, 32, 40

D
drop in, 14, 16–18, 19, 24, 26

E
elbow pads, 10, 12
escalator, 8
extension, 8

F
flatbottom, 8
frontside airs, 37–39
frontside kick flips, 42–43
frontside rock-and-rolls, 39—40

G
grinds, 8, 18, 21–22, 28, 32, 33
  50-50 grinds, 24, 29–31
  scratcher grinds, 22

H
half-pipe manners, 10
helmet, 10, 12

hip, 9

I
inverts, 29

K
kick flips, 36
kick turns, 19–21, 28
knee pads, 10, 12
knee slides, 12–14, 18

M
manual, 26
Masonite, 7–8
mini half-pipe, 9

N
natural obstacles, 6

O
ollie, 32, 33–34, 37, 42
ollie blunt, 40–42
ollie to fakie, 40

P
parking lots, 6
plywood, 7
pop out, 8
Protec, 12
pumping, 14–16, 18

R
ramps, 12, 14, 19
Rector company, 12

About the Author

Justin Hocking lives and skateboards in New York City. He is also an editor of the book *Life and Limb: Skateboarders Write from the Deep End*, published in 2004 by Soft Skull Press.

Credits

All photos © Tony Donaldson/Icon SMI/The Rosen Publishing Group, except p. 4 © Steve Boyle/NewSport/Corbis

Designer: Les Kanturek; Editor: Nicholas Croce;
Photo Research: Fernanda Rocha